Can You Feel It?

Mason V. Bell

BookLeaf
Publishing

India | USA | UK

Presentation by *BookLeaf Publishing*

Web: www.bookleafpub.com

E-mail: info@bookleafpub.com

ISBN: 978-93-5744-363-0

First edition 2022

DEDICATION

To my Dad who gave me the gift of, and love for creative writing. I miss you very much. To my Grandmother who loved me, and helped my mother raise me. Thank you for never hurting me, and for laughing with me and all my silliness. I wish you were here to read this.

ACKNOWLEDGEMENT

Mrs. Jarvis who believes in me to this day, and started believing in me long before I ever started believing in myself. Thank you.
Jonell you've been my biggest supporter through all of this, thank you for being my first ear to all my working pieces. I wouldn't have done this without you.

PREFACE

My passion for poetry and this book stem from my will to bring people with mental health struggles together. I want to give people an outlet and safe place to feel what they feel without judgment. I hope to accomplish giving people a voice when they can't find the words, and a friend with empathy, even if our only unity is in acknowledgment and love.

Beginnings

New beginnings keep me breathing,
right when I hit my fork in the road,
when I feel as though I can't take another second
of this place.
The seasons change refreshing my palate,
hope courses through my veins.
Excitement for recreation and brand new flavors
sparks me back to life,
starting with a count down,
ending with a light show.
I might have missed focused on the one
happening in my body
from a kiss,
a night,
a moment of complete bliss,
leading me into the New Years existence.

A day that's all I have left, to the start of that
perfect,
beautiful new year.
A day that weighs heavy on my soul,
for the hell that seemed to drag along within
every hour of the last 9 months.
How do beautiful things turn so ugly?

Life into death,
living things rotting away….
That's what I'm left drowning in.
At the start,
hope leading me along,
believing,
I thought I knew,
about new.
Only to realize nothing I believed was true, and I
had to learn to retract and retrace the moments I
missed,
or miss understood.
I had to go back and dig through the rubble of
messes I was trapped in,
and the messes I made.
I went to the past,
and at the start there was so much love,
and by the end it was all lost.
Now I'm trying to understand where it all went
wrong.
After a year all I want is closure for my start and
finish.

Isolation

Tic….. tic….. tic….. toc, it's been quiet here.
The only sound besides the clock,
is the quieting rhythmic beat in my chest,
and the weak puffs from my decrepit lungs.
The chilling presence of ghosts,
is louder then my footsteps,
through this dark empty home.
I feel like I've been left here alone for centuries.
What's happening to me?
I forgot how to say hello and goodbye,
what does shaking hands mean?
what does it mean to see someone later?
This is the first cup of coffee I've had with
another set of eyes,
attached to another head,
that isn't my own,
In so long.
Their looks could melt me,
especially with them sitting that close,
I can see the color in their eyes.
6 more feet and they'd look like a stranger to
me.
They gave me a hug when our coffee was done.
Hugs,

I forgot how warm they were
how safe I felt in one.
The way there arms seem just long enough,
or maybe it's that I'm just small enough to fit in
them perfectly.
My skin seems to come alive to their transmitted
electricity,
my hairs rising on end.
For the first time sense I can't remember when
I'm starting to feel alive again.
They just said see you later, and the scary thing
is,
I believe them.

Oh Counselor

Have you ever built a monument? Or pieced together a shattered relic? I once built a marble carving of my soul, I spent years molding it into a perfectly smooth masterpiece. I sat, at the shattered glass, of my future, present, and past. I put each piece back together as if it were a million piece puzzle. The only assistance I requested was another set of eyes, to see what I couldn't, or know what I didn't, to assist in some minor direction. I trusted my counselor, my advisor, for time unmeasured they loyally sat by my side. Then I found them secretly plotting against me, when the floor fell right out from under me, and I went down with all my hard work. All of it imploded, leaving behind more rubble than before. Sitting in the after math, stating I was fine, I was okay. I wouldn't let this drive me insane, only to find, in do time, this was the beginning of the end of my life.

Oasis

Over coffee we meet again, I've never felt so connected. I've told you all about the shattered floor, and the hole I'm falling through. You tell me it can't be true 'those Assholes', 'what can we do?' You tell me to keep on going, to keep on hoping, and start again. I tell you I won't trust anyone, from now on I'm on my own, I'd rather do it all alone. I don't think either of us, could have ever known.

We created our own oasis, hiding from the deadly places. We came to care only for each other, the rest of the world we left to it's plunder. We mapped out treasure hunts, for recent times to come. It became the only part of my day where I didn't shut down and become numb. The time I spend with you has become the only thing that I love.

Erosion

The erosion eating away at my brain, finally made way to the part of me that keeps me sane. I held the door closed fighting the crazy that wanted in, but now that part of me is broken. All that hell I've been holding back busted through, flooding my brain, now I'm insane. I laughed until I cried, and I cried until I laughed. I was breathless and gagging on my insanity, wishing to be free from the psychotic break that now caged me. Looking back I now understand, that choosing to pretend that I was unaffected, by the chaos of the shadows that were growing all around me, until I was trapped in the darkness. Telling you, telling them, telling me, I'm fine, I'm fine…. I'm fine…. Caused this concussive impact of reality. I'm not fine! and not excepting that, and not getting help, resulted in losing myself

Fogging Reality

Fear fogs up my glasses, and my dreams steal
me away,
as I drift through their wishful seas.
It seems as though I'm stuck in this mystified
state,
unable to see clearly.
What is reality?
You want to whisk me away on a splendid
adventure,
and I'm desperate to go,
in my dreams imagining all the wonderful
possibilities. Unclaimed treasure,
lost cities,
new constellations,
and the sent of sweet spring flowers.
Endless moments of laughter,
and perfect moments, that I'll collage in my
memories.
An endless film reel,
and slideshow of seconds, hours,
and minutes we'll spend together.
On the other hand, looking at it again through
my glasses.
I'm clumsy and I break everything I touch,

despite my best efforts.
My family says I'm to sensitive,
I'm described as extra dramatic,
I've become mentally and emotionally
exhausted.
I won't admit it,
to myself or anyone else,
but I've gone through something traumatic.
Ha!
look at me!
I'm barely functioning,
I'm a train wreck waiting to happen,
and deep down I know it, but I can't tell you
that.
Plus,
maybe this adventure is just what I need.
I know I can be a lot…..
and yet,
you said that you couldn't live without me…..

Constructed Zombie

In May I put myself out there for the first time
ever, the date was enchanting, when they kissed
me, butterflies danced through flames inside my
chest. They held me close,
and their fingers played through my long
luscious hair.
A short night of sweet bliss, turned into an
infinite hell, starting with an unforgettable kiss.
I'm not sure what I missed, but the next day they
treated me as if I was diseased,
as if I'd done something unforgivable.
All I wanted was to understand,
what I did to inspire those feelings.
Instead the sexually abused,
became the sexually accused.
I almost lost my job,
but instead I lost myself worth.
When they're friends,
who became my friends told me the truth.
I didn't end up being the rebound they hoped
for,
I wouldn't be,
the empty sex getaway they wanted.
They couldn't have real feelings for me,

because I'm not a Barbie.
Everything they said to me that night was a lie.
The feelings I had that evening,
every intimate touch we shared,
now felt like deceit,
clinging to my body and my brain.
I wanted out of my own skin,
out of my own mind.
I've never felt so dirty inside and out.
I want to hide from myself, now when I look in
the mirror it's covered in filth. Please somebody
explain this pain to me,
it doesn't seem real,
or necessary.
I called my best friend everyday,
trying to make sense of the things that were
happening to me,
but I guess that was wrong, because they've
stopped answering all my calls. Turns out the
best way to handle life is to do it numb, and by
yourself.
I take what my doctor prescribed,
to help me feel nothing inside.
I fill my schedule with endless hours of work,
and theater.
I don't give a single second to myself,
and the result is I'm all better.
Turns out the answer was simple,

be a zombie,
and that will be the closest version of happily
sane.

Now That Your Gone

When you left, I packed up all the things that
made up us,
our love for each other,
the moments we shared.
I put them in a box,
and stuck them in the darkest part of my closet,
like a nightmare I wanted to forget.
Pretending, that because I left it in the abyss of
that dark closet,
it wouldn't haunt me in the back of my mind at
every turn, when I wasn't distracted by everyday
life. I couldn't scroll through pictures on my
phone, scared that I'd bump into you.
All that captured wonder,
one glance meant no more forgetting, no more
pretending.
That you didn't exist,
that it doesn't hurt,
that my heart doesn't die, every time I whisper
the truth hidden in my mind. That I loved you,
and still do, and will for the rest of my life.
Devastatingly, that doesn't mean I'll have you in
my life,

or that I'll get to see you again, in anything more
then a picture.
For you said goodbye, and I didn't even get the
chance.
That's modern day life isn't it?
To end years of long hours spent with someone
special to you,
in one small sentence. On a small hand held
device, that can make me hold my breath,
weep and cry,
because someone uses it to say goodbye.
No last farewell hug, no warning,
just a swiftly pulled out rug, that without a
second thought someone tugged.

Now that I've had some time, and I've walked
down the road of reality.
I unpack that far away hidden box, from that
black hole of monsters where I stashed it.
I've realized, that's the only part of you I get to
keep,
it's the only part I still have in my life.
Even though the rejection hurts,
the affections we shared are twice its worth.
I want to remember I love you,
even if you've chosen to have forgotten.
I won't I'll remember there were more smiles
then tears,

more love than hate.
I'll remember that my love for you, was worth
the pain of us being human,
and that my will to fight for you, will never be in
vein, though it try's to make me insane.
I didn't sweat or bleed begrudgingly, I was
fulfilled whole heartedly in my labor of love for
you.
I unpack the things from that box, because I
can't imagine a world where I don't have you in
my life.
I'll live with the memories,
that way I don't have to LIVE without you, after
all without you I don't really want to.

Goodbye

Echos in my soul and heavy weighted shadows
cling to me,
my aching chest,
and numbing skin.
My haunted heart is bleeding through,
there's no hiding the loss of you.
I drown my days filling every second,
in every minute,
consuming each hour.
Hiding in it,
day after day,
then weeks have passed into months,
but it never lasts,
soon enough I can't keep up,
and the pain of losing us resurfaces.
The throb breaks my bones,
with every labored breath.
My memory of you is concussive like a nuclear
blast,
my soul is left trembling from impact,
and my heart died with the unspoken goodbye
that was never left.

Whispers of real loves meaning chase me,
saying it's letting go,
it's shameless in every way,
for me, real love is never forgetting.
Close to my heart I save a book of songs I would
have sent you,
if you hadn't left without saying goodbye.

Moving Shadows

There's a terrifying shadow following me,
I've tried to scare them off,
I've tried to outrun them.
I even tried to report them to the authorities, but
like an unnerving stalker they follow me
relentlessly,
endlessly,
and I'm worried one day they'll take me and kill
me.
I know who they are,
I know their face,
I fear them more than any other.
Hate is the shadow that clings to me like a
parasite,
trying to over take me.
That's what failed love does,
it leaves you diseased and sick,
waiting for Hate to overtake its new weakened
domain.
I'd give in,
but I'm to stubborn,
and here I am fighting against the inevitable.
One day I won't run hard enough,
and just like that I'll be gone,
overcome by the shadows I run from.

The Cost of Survival

She's covered in marks and ruins,
she has more burns and cuts then she knows how
to patch up,
and she treads sinking sand pointlessly as it
swallows her whole.
In a matter of days,
hours,
moments,
this girl has lost her best friend.
Watched a promise turn to ash,
been used like a tool,
and then abused.
Her abuser,
becoming the next closest thing
to a best friend,
for she's all alone.
She starts building a master piece,
only to hit road block,
after road block.
She tells a lie to keep it alive,
only for it to continue to die. She shouts begging
to be heard,
she holds up the world with all her might,
only to be told she's not holding it right.

That's to low you'renot holding it high enough,
she has no control as she's yanked from side to
side,
bed,
to floor,
to sky.
Then everything she loves,
and knows turns to infection,
cutting her off in a Quarantine zone.
Grim whispers he's coming for the next one,
the ones most beloved by her, and the only one
left that compiled her existence.
She screams
wishing he'd come for her, and set her free, so
she doesn't have to bear witness, doesn't have to
see.
The fire of life eats up all that imbodies her
universe, with hate and pride, rejection and
sickness.
Its all stealing her will for existence.

For Me

Why do I torture myself like this? How do all
my decisions end up being self destructive?
I caught a feeling for them, they said they felt
the same, and we decided to date, but it became
pretty clear early on I just wasn't the one.
I let them go, and yet I still can't help, but feel as
though I'll never be enough for someone to love.
I let my friends convince me to try online dating,
what a disastrous night. The world seems to sync
to a beat differently then me,
I wasn't interested in sleeping with a stranger,
and yet they wouldn't stop kissing me,
and I couldn't escape.
That beautiful date I had in mind turned into my
personal nightmare.
I'm sick of dating, I'm tired of people.
I'm done with my own body, feeling violated,
and abused.
How do I constantly get stuck in these hellish
situations?
Now I just want out of my body,
I want to forget what it feels like to not want to
be touched,
and it being forced on me.

I can't believe they think it's okay to say that
kind of objectifying thing to me. That's sexual
harassment, I'm sick of it.
I shouldn't feel like I need to where baggy
clothes, to feel safe to go outside,
and be under humanity's eye.
Forget physical touch,
and my physical outlook.
I'm sick of this emotion based shit,
I don't want be friends with them.
They're not my best friend! They're not even
my real friend,
and yet they force me to introduce us like that to
everybody,
and if this is how I'm feeling about them.
How can I be their best friend?
It doesn't even make sense.
How did I get stuck being the savior for
someone I've never even loved?
I wish the world would stop forcing me into its
conformity's,
that checklist that makes up my identity,
people forcing there friendship, and physical
needs on to me.
I'm done I'm setting myself free,
no more lying to them,
I can't do this friendship with them,
and I won't.

I won't date anyone else, unless I can choose,
and trust it's worth the risks,
of the costs,
of a relationship.
I'm gonna be me! Frankly I don't give two shits
what you strangers think of me, I'm doing
what's best for me.
No more emotional or,
physical traps.
Starting with the drugs that keep me numb,
I deserve to feel and grow,
at a rate that's normal for me,
I was never meant to be exactly the same as
somebody else.
I'm un-caging myself and spreading my wings,
this is what's best for me. Finally!

I Forgot What It Was To Feel

My world is shattered glass,
I keep trying to put it back together piece by
piece,
but all I do is cut myself on its jagged broken
edges.
My blood floods the glass in front of me,
hopelessness and despair grab my heart like a
vice grip.
I want to die so bad I pick out all the ways I
could leave peacefully,
but a stronger part of me fights, keeping me
barely alive and miserable.
I could scream endlessly, trying to be free, but
all I do is relieve the pressure inside me, just
enough to keep me
From exploding inside.

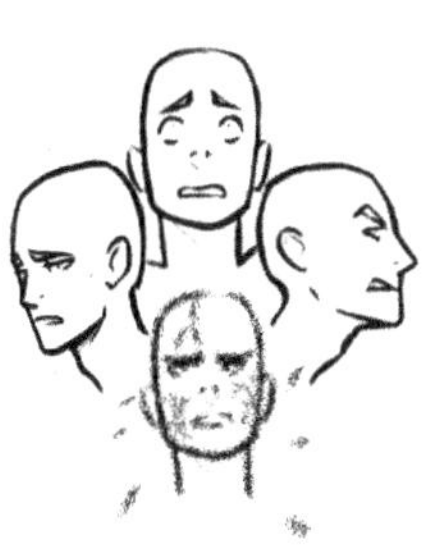

If Only

I wish the world was different,
I wish your parents raised you to believe that no
love is different,
that love is love, and as long as we all simply
love,
the world will be simply happy.
Maybe we'd know what it was like to not feel
alone,
you wouldn't repress that side of yourself, and I
wouldn't have been made to believe that I was
unnatural.
Instead we'd stargaze,
and share long warm embraces,
and we wouldn't spend the rest of our lives
hiding our faces.
Now we'll never know what we could have
been,
even if it was destined to be,
or merely content and happy.

Kindred Spirits

I don't want to replace you.
You see I think your exceptional,
and funny.
You make up the best parts of a human being,
and I just want to exist in the same space as you.
The same way I want to exist next to ocean
waves,
on soft sandy shores,
under clear night sky's.
Listening and watching the world fall and rise.

Fresh Starts

There's an opportunity ahead of me to escape,
this small mountain of history,
I've been fumbling through for to much time.
It's only an ocean away,
but I'm happy to say it feels as though it's a
world away. A safe place for me to start fresh,
grow my own fields and crops,
I can build my home out of rocks if I so want.
It's perfect for me, after all it's new.
I don't know if I'll succeed at being the person I
desire to be,
but right now I'm allowing myself the
opportunity to find out.
Maybe success is really just taking a chance,
even with the risk of it ending up being
nothing more than a much needed trip.
You'll never break new ground,
if you don't work the dirt for the seeds you want
to take root into the earth.
Not all gardens grow,
but you'll never know,
if they would have,
if you don't give them the chance to thrive,

before deciding that they have already died.

I have my favorite shoes, worn photos of the
ones I love,
a jacket for brisk days,
and an open mind for everything new I'm about
to find.
I'm completely ready.
My only lost wish is that I could have shared
this with you, and knowing that I can't,
causes me to really miss you.
Taking one last goodbye glance I board that
rocket ship to a new a galaxy, where I can start
doing what's best for me. I can't wait to see the
person I'll grow up to be.

Missing you

I reckon,
that I wish I didn't miss you anymore,
for the wavering in my heart is often more then I
can bare.
I find myself lost in my wistful thoughts of you,
you had such an essences,
I long for the brilliant way you carried your
fragrance.
It started in your room it was rich with incense,
like sitting in the sea breeze,
or lolling through a lavender field.
A place where you close your eyes,
and let your nose guide you, and take you away.
Your room welcomed me into that with ease, it
was rich and warm.
You smelled like earth after a first rain,
and herbs freshly picked oiling the tips of my
fingers,
with a scent I hoped would last forever,
and like cinnamon and nutmeg thrown on my
latte.
The scent of your existence was treasure to me,
it was cozier than home and even more of an
enigma than space.

Your soul was a kaleidoscope,
ever beautiful,
and in constant motion of gorgeous vastness and
color.
I miss the time I would spend in your fruitful
mind,
it was such a enchanting garden with many
flowers,
fruits,
and veggies;
and my God those ideas you'd turn to jelly's and
extravagant bouquets,
and deliciously marinated dishes.
I could have spent a life time in that garden,
trying all the new things you came up with, and
forever enjoying the recipes we had at our
disposal all the time.
Your heart is what I miss most,
what an extraordinary piece of architecture you
had in there!
The spiral staircases!
The library's and museums of art and culture!
Fascinating!
You could tell that a lot of time had gone into
shaping and molding that stunning marble
structure.

I haven't seen you sense that last lovely visit,
and I haven't heard from you sense that last
goodbye letter.
All I hope is that I didn't break your heart,
and crack that perfectly imperfect castle that is
all that you are.

I Hope You Know

49

Sometimes I feel like a code writer subtly putting my deep thoughts in every word, wondering if you'll read all these poems I write for you? Wondering if you can tell which ones they are? If you notice the coding I've strung through just for you? But the truth is I don't know if you read my stories, or if you'd just rather not know or see anything that has to do with me. Which is a shame, because I got to say a lot of big beautiful things in these pieces of art, that I've only dreamed and wished I could have expressed and said to you. What's a poet to do? I simply keep writing in code for you.

Lost in Translation

When we parted ways, words were spoken on your end, and I was left with silence. The goodbye you left sent my heart and head drowning in what you said, I hurt you, I was un empathetic. You weren't my home! Or savior! Or my therapist! And now you weren't my friend, but that's the crazy part.

I am empathetic! And I was to that situation, and you were right I never intended to hurt you, and if you'd only expressed to me the way my actions were making you feel, I would have apologized. I would have grown, and I would have had a better understanding of how to love you right. I never saw you as a therapist, or a savior, I saw you as my best friend. I guess in that sense, I did view you as a home, and I'm sorry for that because it's clearly not what you wanted, but I think deep down you know I never viewed you as someone who needed to save me. I merely viewed you, as that person I asked if they wanted to come along for the ride. It doesn't matter now though it's all gone, your gone. Even so, I still think about you all the time. I wonder how your doing? I wonder if your sisters doing better? If your brother still gaslights you? How are there little ones? Are they still dancing and singing? Is your other brother still in the honeymoon phase of his marriage? Was the ceremony beautiful? Did you hate it or love it? I think about your mom all the time, I'm always wondering how her and your dad are? If they still love there new place on the beach? I wonder and worry if you're all safe from the chaos of COVID-19? I think about you mostly and your fur babies. Do you finally feel at home that close to salty waves? Did you find anymore rocks that fascinate you, and move you? What about any new music that blows your mind? That you have to get lost in, or the words grip your heart and soul so much you carry them where ever you go. Have you read any new books? Have any of them been brilliant? Or are the authors completely torturing you again? Have you still been doing art? I still think your art work would make an amazing gallery show, you are so brilliant and your art is so captivating. Does your home still smell the same? Are you feeding yourself? Are you sleeping? How's the little ghost? How's Lilith and Rue? How are you? Are you still taking the space you need? Are people still giving it to you? You may have said goodbye for all your reasons, but I'm still here for all my own. I genuinely love you and care about you, and see you. The heartbreaking thing for me, is I feel like we both went through all this pain, for a devastating moment of lost translation.

Their World

They were human and yet I've never met anyone
quite like them.
They had their own ecosystem I found alluring,
and I was constantly drawn there.
It gave me euphoria to be in that place breath the
air of their space,
they had all their own galaxy's and stars and
constellations.
Their own legends, hero's and gods.
I loved their oceans more than ours, and the
creatures there were more favorable, and
mystical.
When I would visit I'd bring them gifts;
I did my best to build up their home and add
more beauty to it,
but at the end of the day my skin and the air I
breathed was toxic to their environment.
To protect their home they formed a shell that
cast a beautiful silver glow,
without a goodbye or a farewell I was never
welcome there again.

I often find myself sitting at the edge of my
world,
starring at that beautiful silver hue missing them
and their world,
wishing for the real goodbye I never got.

Letting Go

I think it's safe to say that there are things in life
that stick with us forever,
like the first time we ask our parents about the
stars.
The first time we fall in love,
our first kiss,
graduation,
our 21st birthdays....
or at least we remember not wanting to
remember that one.
We always remember and hold on,
while simultaneously remembering to let go.
Some things are easier to let go then others,
I've never completely let go of the loved ones I
lost.
They always stay with me in my heart,
I can hold on to that little echo deep inside,
when I feel down,
or start doubting myself.
The whispers,
of their silenced voices keep telling me to never
give up.
It's time to let go of this year,
I have weeks left until the next one starts,

and I can't take this one with me,
the costs would be two realities colliding.
The results of that would be losing myself in the
past,
while trying to exist in the present.
To be ready for the new to come,
I have to make room to grow.
After all I'm still learning,
and deciding who it is I want to be when I grow
up.
Truth is I don't know yet,
but if I'm gonna find out,
I can't focus on all the things I'm holding onto.
it's time to let this year go,
It's time to let them go.
It's hard sometimes to say goodbye without
closure,
and I've spent most my year grasping for it.
As I slid into a dark pit,
but what I found,
is life doesn't always give us closure.
Maybe my closure,
is having closure in knowing that there isn't any,
and maybe letting go and saying goodbye
finally.
Is me telling them,
and myself,
I'll always remember,

and I'll never forget.

I'll certainly still miss them,
but I'm gonna keep going,
keep moving.
I'll take a picture of this moment,
this spot,
and in that sense I'll always look back,
but I'll keep taking steps;
until this road leads me to farther places.
I won't stay here,
at the fork of what could have been,
and what is,
but instead I'll strive to move forward.
I'll think about how bright the light was,
from that shooting star,
as I made my biggest wish, on that beautiful
light the night it died.
All it's brightness,
lit the way,
for the path I'm about to take.

www.ingramcontent.com/pod-product-compliance
Lightning Source LLC
LaVergne TN
LVHW021231200726
843509LV00012B/1471